Amy Dowden: The Dancer Who Dared to Dream

Early Life and Passion for Dance
Born on August 10, 1990, in Caerphilly, Wales, Amy Dowden's love for dance began at the tender age of eight. Growing up with a twin sister and an older brother, Amy's childhood was filled with the rhythmic beats of ballroom and Latin American dance. The vibrant Welsh countryside of Caerphilly provided a picturesque backdrop for her budding passion.

Rising Through the Ranks
Amy's journey to stardom was anything but ordinary. Partnering with Ben Jones, she soared to new heights in the dance world. The dynamic duo became British Open Latin Dance Champions in 2017, marking the first all-British pair to win the championship in over 30 years. Their impressive list of accolades includes titles such as British Dance Federation Champions, English Closed Champions, and Welsh Closed and Open Champions. Amy also earned the distinction of being a four-time British National Finalist and a World Championship semi-finalist, cementing her status as one of the UK's highest-ranking ballroom and Latin dancers.

Stepping into the Spotlight

Amy's talent caught the eye of the BBC, and in 2017, she became the first Welsh professional dancer to join the cast of the beloved television show "Strictly Come Dancing." Her debut series saw her paired with comedian Brian Conley, with the pair dancing their way to week five. Each subsequent season brought new challenges and triumphs:

Series 16: Partnered with actor Danny John-Jules, their energetic performances and a notable jive earned them the first perfect score of the season.

Series 17: Amy reached the finals with TV presenter Karim Zeroual, dazzling audiences with their chemistry and precision.

Series 18: Teaming up with TV presenter JJ Chalmers, they finished in 6th place.

Series 19: Amy partnered with musician Tom Fletcher, facing challenges including a bout of COVID-19 that temporarily took them off the dance floor.

Series 20: Her journey with EastEnders actor James Bye ended in week 6.

Christmas Special 2022: Amy danced with CBeebies presenter George Webster, adding festive cheer to her repertoire.

Dance Tours and Professional Engagements
Beyond the "Strictly" stage, Amy headlined her own tour, "Here Come The Girls," alongside fellow dancers Dianne Buswell and Chloe Hewitt in 2019. She has been a staple on the "Strictly Come Dancing Live!" tour since 2018, delighting fans across the country. Notably, she performed with Karim Zeroual on tour in 2020, continuing their on-screen partnership.

Amy and Ben Jones also share a personal and professional bond, as they run the Art in Motion dance school in Cradley Heath, West Midlands, nurturing the next generation of dancers.

Personal Struggles and Triumphs
Amy's journey hasn't been without its challenges. She has bravely battled Crohn's disease since childhood, openly discussing its impact on her career. Her courage was highlighted in a BBC documentary aired in October 2020, which later won a BAFTA Cymru award.

In May 2023, Amy faced a new challenge: a diagnosis of grade III breast cancer. Undergoing a mastectomy and chemotherapy, she showed immense strength and resilience. Despite contracting sepsis and breaking her foot, she remained determined. By November 2023, Amy had made a courageous cameo on "Strictly" without her wig, embodying hope and perseverance.

February 2024 brought a glimmer of relief, as Amy announced her latest check-up showed no signs of cancer, though she would need five years to be declared fully clear. Her indomitable spirit shone through as she looked forward to returning to the "Strictly" dance floor.

Recognitions and Honours

Amy Dowden's contributions to dance and her efforts to raise awareness about inflammatory bowel disease were recognized in 2024 when she was appointed a Member of the Order of the British Empire (MBE). This honor underscores her impact not only as a dancer but also as an advocate and inspirational figure.

Conclusion

Amy Dowden's story is one of passion, resilience, and unwavering determination. From a young girl in Caerphilly to a celebrated dancer on the international stage, her journey continues to inspire. With a bright future ahead, Amy's dance and life stories are far from over, promising more captivating performances and personal triumphs.

Amy Dowden: The Dancer Who Dared to Dream

In the small town of Caerphilly, Wales, a young girl named Amy Dowden twirled around her living room, her heart beating to the rhythm of a dream. Born on August 10, 1990, Amy's early years were filled with the joy and chaos of growing up with a twin sister and an older brother. From the moment she could walk, she danced, her movements echoing the vibrant energy of the Welsh countryside that surrounded her home.

The Birth of a Passion

At the age of eight, Amy's parents enrolled her in a local dance class. What began as a pastime quickly blossomed into a consuming passion. The dance floor became her world, a place where she could express herself in ways words never could. Her talent was undeniable, and soon she was partnering with Ben Jones, a pairing that would change her life forever.

A Journey of Triumphs

Amy and Ben's chemistry on the dance floor was electric. Together, they conquered the British dance scene, becoming the British Open Latin Dance Champions in 2017. This victory was monumental, marking them as the first all-British pair to win the championship in over 30 years. Their triumphs didn't stop there; they were also crowned British Dance Federation Champions, English Closed Champions, and Welsh Closed and Open Champions. With each title, Amy's star shone brighter.

Stepping into the Limelight

In 2017, Amy's talent took her from the dance halls of Britain to the bright lights of television. She became the first Welsh professional dancer to join the cast of the BBC's "Strictly Come Dancing." Her debut on the show was nothing short of magical. Paired with comedian Brian Conley, Amy's infectious energy and grace captured the hearts of millions. They danced their way through five thrilling weeks, and though they didn't win, Amy's journey on "Strictly" was just beginning.

Over the next few years, Amy's dance card was filled with a series of unforgettable partnerships:

2018: With actor Danny John-Jules, Amy delivered performances that left audiences in awe, including a jive that scored the season's first perfect 10.
2019: Partnered with TV presenter Karim Zeroual, Amy reached the finals, their dazzling routines earning them a perfect 40 for their jive.
2020: Television presenter JJ Chalmers danced with Amy to a commendable sixth-place finish.
2021: Musician Tom Fletcher and Amy faced the challenges of COVID-19, yet their resilience saw them through to week nine.
2022: Amy danced with EastEnders actor James Bye, their journey ending in week six but leaving a lasting impression.
Amy's talent wasn't confined to the main show. She also brought festive joy to the "Strictly Come Dancing Christmas Special," dancing with CBeebies presenter George Webster.

Tours and Beyond

Amy's passion for dance extended beyond the "Strictly" stage. In 2019, she headlined the "Here Come The Girls" tour with fellow dancers Dianne Buswell and Chloe Hewitt, captivating audiences across the country. She also became a regular on the "Strictly Come Dancing Live!" tour, where in 2020, she reunited with Karim Zeroual to delight fans live.

Alongside her professional achievements, Amy and Ben Jones nurtured the next generation of dancers at their Art in Motion dance school in Cradley Heath, West Midlands.

Personal Battles and Triumphs

Behind the glitter and glamor of the dance floor, Amy faced personal battles with courage and grace. Since childhood, she had lived with Crohn's disease, a condition that posed significant challenges to her dancing career. In May 2019, Amy spoke openly about her struggles, and in October 2020, her story was featured in a BBC documentary, which won a BAFTA Cymru award.

In May 2023, Amy's resilience was tested again when she was diagnosed with grade III breast cancer. She underwent a mastectomy and chemotherapy, facing each day with the same tenacity that had made her a dance champion. Despite contracting sepsis and breaking her foot, Amy remained hopeful. By November 2023, she made a brave cameo on "Strictly," appearing without her wig and inspiring millions.

A Beacon of Hope

February 2024 brought a beacon of hope: Amy's latest check-up showed no signs of cancer. Although she won't be given the all-clear for five years, her spirit remains undimmed. She looks forward to returning to the "Strictly" dance floor, ready to create more magic.

Amy Dowden's contributions to dance and her advocacy for inflammatory bowel disease awareness were recognized in 2024 when she was appointed a Member of the Order of the British Empire (MBE). This honor celebrated her as a dancer, an advocate, and an inspirational figure.

Conclusion

Amy Dowden's story is a testament to the power of dreams, resilience, and unyielding passion. From a young girl dancing in her living room to a celebrated star on the international stage, Amy's journey continues to inspire. Her story is far from over, promising more captivating performances and personal triumphs. With every step, twirl, and leap, Amy Dowden dances her way into the hearts of many, a true beacon of hope and talent.

Facing the Future with Hope
As Amy Dowden stands on the threshold of her future, her story is a tapestry of triumphs, trials, and the unwavering spirit of a dancer who refuses to be defined by adversity. Her journey is not just about the accolades and titles but also about the resilience and hope that shine through even the darkest moments.

Dancing Through Adversity
Despite the challenges, Amy's love for dance never waned. When she announced her intention to return to "Strictly Come Dancing" in the upcoming series, the news was met with widespread excitement and support. For Amy, dancing is not just a profession; it is a lifeline, a way to express her innermost self and to connect with others.

Her return to the dance floor is highly anticipated, not only for the incredible performances she is known for but also for the powerful message she embodies: that strength and beauty can emerge from struggle. Amy's story is a beacon of hope for anyone facing their own battles, proving that with passion and perseverance, one can overcome the most daunting obstacles.

The Next Chapter

As Amy prepares for her comeback, she continues to inspire through her advocacy and her personal story. She actively raises awareness about Crohn's disease and breast cancer, sharing her experiences to help others understand and cope with these conditions. Her openness and honesty have made her a role model, showing that vulnerability and strength can coexist beautifully.

In the dance studio, Amy and Ben Jones remain committed to their students at Art in Motion. They teach not just the technical aspects of dance but also the values of dedication, resilience, and joy that have defined Amy's career. Their school is a testament to the couple's love for dance and their desire to pass on their passion to the next generation.

A Legacy of Inspiration

Amy Dowden's journey is a story of unwavering determination and boundless enthusiasm. Her achievements on the dance floor are matched by her courage off it, creating a legacy that goes beyond the world of dance. She has shown that true champions are those who rise above their challenges and continue to shine, no matter how difficult the path.

As she looks to the future, Amy's spirit remains unbreakable. With her health improving and her return to "Strictly" on the horizon, there is a sense of anticipation and excitement. Fans and fellow dancers alike are eager to see what she will achieve next, knowing that whatever she does, it will be infused with the same passion and grace that have defined her journey.

Conclusion

Amy Dowden's life story is one of inspiration, resilience, and unwavering passion. From her early days in Caerphilly to the grand stages of international dance competitions, and from the "Strictly Come Dancing" ballroom to her battles with illness, Amy has faced every challenge with courage and grace. Her journey continues to inspire countless others, proving that with determination and love for what you do, anything is possible. As Amy dances into the future, her story remains a testament to the power of dreams and the strength of the human spirit.

A New Chapter: Embracing the Future
Amy Dowden's story is far from over. As she steps back onto the "Strictly Come Dancing" stage, she brings with her not just the elegance and skill of a seasoned professional but also the depth and resilience of someone who has faced life's toughest battles and emerged stronger. The audience awaits her return with bated breath, eager to witness her triumphant comeback.

Sharing Her Journey
Throughout her journey, Amy has remained committed to sharing her story, knowing that her experiences can provide comfort and inspiration to others. She continues to advocate for those living with Crohn's disease and breast cancer, using her platform to raise awareness and support for these causes. Her openness about her health struggles has touched many lives, offering a beacon of hope to those facing similar challenges.

Expanding Her Influence

Beyond the dance floor, Amy is exploring new ways to make an impact. She is working on a book that chronicles her life, from her early days in Wales to her rise to fame on "Strictly," and the personal battles she has fought along the way. The book promises to be a source of inspiration, filled with anecdotes, lessons learned, and the unyielding spirit that has carried her through.

Amy is also considering taking on speaking engagements, where she can share her story with live audiences, spreading her message of resilience and hope. Her goal is to reach as many people as possible, encouraging them to pursue their passions and face their fears with courage.

Building a Lasting Legacy

At Art in Motion, Amy and Ben are more dedicated than ever to nurturing young talent. They continue to mentor aspiring dancers, teaching them not just the technical skills needed to excel but also the importance of perseverance and maintaining a positive outlook, no matter what obstacles life throws their way. Their dance school has become a haven for young dancers, a place where dreams are cultivated and lifelong friendships are formed.

The Support of Loved Ones

Through all of her ups and downs, Amy's family and friends have been her rock. Her twin sister and older brother, along with Ben, have provided unwavering support, celebrating her successes and comforting her during difficult times. This close-knit support system has been crucial to her resilience, giving her the strength to keep moving forward.

Looking Forward

As Amy looks to the future, she does so with a renewed sense of purpose and excitement. She is determined to continue dancing, advocating, and inspiring others. Her story is a reminder that even in the face of adversity, one can find the strength to dance through life's challenges.

Conclusion

Amy Dowden's journey is a remarkable tale of passion, resilience, and triumph. From her early days in Caerphilly to her stardom on "Strictly Come Dancing" and her brave battles with health issues, she has shown the world what it means to persevere with grace. Her legacy is one of inspiration, touching countless lives through her dance, her advocacy, and her unwavering spirit. As she steps into the next chapter of her life, Amy Dowden continues to shine as a beacon of hope, proving that with determination and love, anything is possible.

Triumphs on the Horizon
As Amy Dowden embarks on the next phase of her journey, she does so with a heart full of dreams and a spirit undimmed by the trials she has faced. Her story continues to unfold, each new chapter a testament to her enduring passion for dance and her unyielding resilience.

The Anticipated Return to Strictly
The announcement of Amy's return to "Strictly Come Dancing" has created a buzz of anticipation among fans and fellow dancers alike. Her presence on the show is more than just a return to the spotlight; it symbolizes the triumph of hope over adversity. The upcoming series promises to be a memorable one, with Amy's performances carrying the weight of her journey and the joy of her return to what she loves most.

Spreading Her Wings
Beyond "Strictly," Amy is exploring new ventures that allow her to share her passion and experiences with a wider audience. She has plans to launch a series of online dance tutorials, designed to make dance accessible to everyone, regardless of their background or skill level. These tutorials will not only teach the technical aspects of ballroom and Latin dance but also emphasize the joy and therapeutic benefits of dancing.

Empowering Through Storytelling
Amy's upcoming book is eagerly awaited by her fans and the general public. It promises to be a heartfelt account of her life, filled with the highs and lows that have shaped her into the person she is today. Through her writing, Amy aims to inspire others to follow their dreams and face their challenges with courage. Her story, told in her own words, is sure to be a source of strength and inspiration for many.

Giving Back to the Community
Amy and Ben's commitment to their dance school, Art in Motion, remains unwavering. They have introduced scholarship programs to provide opportunities for underprivileged children to learn dance, ensuring that financial barriers do not stand in the way of young talent. The couple is also planning to organize community dance events, fostering a love for dance and creating a supportive and inclusive environment for all participants.

A Voice for Health Advocacy
Amy continues to use her platform to raise awareness about Crohn's disease and breast cancer. She collaborates with health organizations to promote early detection and provide support for those living with these conditions. Her involvement in health advocacy extends to public speaking engagements, where she shares her journey and offers hope to others facing similar battles.

The Support Network

Throughout her journey, Amy's family, friends, and fans have played a crucial role in her resilience. Their unwavering support has been a constant source of strength, reminding her that she is never alone in her struggles. Amy's gratitude for her support network is immeasurable, and she often credits them for her ability to keep moving forward.

Dancing into the Future

With her health showing positive signs and her return to dance imminent, Amy Dowden looks to the future with optimism and excitement. Her journey is a powerful reminder of the human spirit's capacity to overcome adversity and to find beauty in every step, twirl, and leap. As she prepares to grace the "Strictly" stage once more, the world watches in anticipation, ready to be inspired by her courage and her unwavering love for dance.

Conclusion

Amy Dowden's story is one of incredible resilience, boundless passion, and enduring hope. From her beginnings in Caerphilly to the bright lights of "Strictly Come Dancing" and through her battles with health challenges, Amy has shown that true strength lies in the ability to keep dancing, no matter what. Her journey continues to inspire countless individuals, proving that with determination, love, and support, anything is possible. As she steps into her future, Amy Dowden remains a shining example of what it means to live life to the fullest, dancing through every challenge and triumph with grace and joy.

A New Era of Empowerment
As Amy Dowden embraces this new chapter of her life, she does so with a mission to empower others. She has become a symbol of hope and resilience, not just in the world of dance but in the broader community. Her story resonates with people from all walks of life, reminding them that challenges can be transformed into stepping stones toward greater heights.

A Beacon of Inspiration
Amy's story has inspired countless individuals, from young dancers dreaming of the stage to people battling health issues. She frequently receives letters and messages from fans who have found strength in her journey. These heartfelt communications affirm her belief in the power of sharing her story and the importance of being a beacon of hope for others.

Strengthening Advocacy Efforts
Amy's advocacy efforts are expanding. She has partnered with several health organizations to promote awareness and support for Crohn's disease and breast cancer. These collaborations include fundraising events, educational campaigns, and support groups aimed at providing resources and community for those affected by these conditions. Amy's firsthand experience brings authenticity and relatability to her advocacy work, making her a trusted voice in the health community.

Expanding Art in Motion
Art in Motion, the dance school she runs with Ben Jones, continues to flourish. They have plans to expand their curriculum to include dance therapy classes, focusing on the mental and emotional benefits of dance. These classes aim to provide a healing space for individuals dealing with stress, anxiety, and other emotional challenges, using dance as a form of expression and release.

Embracing Technology
Amy and Ben are also exploring the digital realm to reach a global audience. They plan to launch a series of virtual dance workshops, allowing people from around the world to learn from them. These workshops will cover various dance styles and levels, making high-quality dance instruction accessible to everyone, regardless of location.

Personal Growth and Reflection
Amy's personal journey has been one of continuous growth and reflection. She often reflects on the lessons she has learned and the people who have influenced her path. Each experience, whether a victory or a setback, has contributed to her strength and resilience. Amy remains committed to personal growth, embracing new challenges and opportunities with an open heart and a determined spirit.

Looking Forward

As Amy looks to the future, she does so with a renewed sense of purpose. She is determined to make the most of every opportunity, both on and off the dance floor. Her goals include continuing her advocacy work, expanding her dance school, and exploring new ways to inspire and empower others.

Legacy of Love and Resilience

Amy Dowden's legacy is one of love, resilience, and unwavering determination. She has shown that it is possible to face life's greatest challenges with grace and strength. Her journey is a testament to the power of passion and the human spirit's ability to overcome adversity. Amy's story will continue to inspire and uplift, reminding everyone that, no matter the obstacles, it is always possible to dance through life with hope and joy.

Conclusion

Amy Dowden's life is a remarkable journey of passion, perseverance, and inspiration. From her early days in Caerphilly to the grand stages of "Strictly Come Dancing" and beyond, Amy has faced each challenge with courage and grace. Her story is a beacon of hope, encouraging others to pursue their dreams and face their challenges with an indomitable spirit. As she steps into the future, Amy Dowden remains a shining example of what it means to live life fully, embracing every moment with love, resilience, and a commitment to making a positive impact on the world.

Embracing New Horizons
With every step she takes, Amy Dowden continues to break new ground and inspire those around her. Her determination to overcome adversity and her passion for dance have opened up new horizons, both personally and professionally. As she moves forward, Amy is excited to explore these opportunities, knowing that her journey is far from over.

The Launch of Virtual Dance Classes
The virtual dance workshops Amy and Ben are planning are set to launch soon. These classes will bring the joy of dance to living rooms around the world, allowing people to connect with Amy's expertise and enthusiasm from anywhere. The classes will cover a range of styles and skill levels, ensuring that everyone, from beginners to seasoned dancers, can benefit from her guidance. These workshops are a testament to Amy's commitment to making dance accessible to all and to fostering a global dance community.

Expanding the Reach of Advocacy
Amy's advocacy work is expanding in exciting ways. She is developing a series of online resources and webinars to provide information and support for those dealing with Crohn's disease and breast cancer. These resources will include practical advice, personal stories, and expert insights, creating a comprehensive support system for individuals and families affected by these conditions. Amy's goal is to empower others with knowledge and support, helping them navigate their own journeys with confidence and hope.

Collaborations and Partnerships
Amy is also exploring collaborations with other dancers, artists, and advocates. These partnerships aim to create interdisciplinary projects that combine dance with other forms of art and advocacy. One such project includes a dance performance that incorporates storytelling, music, and visual art to raise awareness about health issues and celebrate the resilience of the human spirit. These collaborations highlight Amy's innovative approach and her desire to use her platform for a greater good.

Personal Milestones
Amidst her professional endeavors, Amy is also celebrating personal milestones. Her marriage to Ben Jones continues to be a source of strength and joy. Together, they support each other's dreams and share a deep love for dance and teaching. Their relationship is a beautiful example of partnership, both on and off the dance floor, and it adds a layer of warmth and inspiration to Amy's story.

Reflecting on the Journey
Amy often takes time to reflect on her journey and the incredible support she has received from her family, friends, and fans. These reflections remind her of the importance of gratitude and the power of community. She knows that her achievements are not just the result of her efforts but also the collective support and love of those around her.

Future Aspirations
Looking to the future, Amy has many aspirations. She dreams of choreographing a major dance production, one that tells her story and the stories of others who have faced significant challenges. This production would be a celebration of resilience, hope, and the transformative power of dance. Amy is also considering furthering her education, possibly studying dance therapy or health advocacy to deepen her understanding and broaden her impact.

Conclusion
Amy Dowden's story is one of unending inspiration and resilience. Her journey from a young dancer in Caerphilly to a beloved figure on "Strictly Come Dancing" is marked by passion, perseverance, and a commitment to making a difference. Amy's future is bright with possibilities, and her legacy of hope, strength, and dance continues to grow.

As she steps into new ventures and embraces fresh challenges, Amy remains a beacon of light and a source of inspiration for countless people. Her life is a testament to the power of dreams and the human spirit's ability to overcome adversity. Amy Dowden's story will continue to inspire and uplift, proving that with determination and love, one can dance through any storm and emerge stronger on the other side.

Dancing Through Life's Challenges

As Amy Dowden continues to navigate her path, she does so with a spirit undeterred by the trials she has faced. Her resilience and determination have not only made her a beloved dancer but also a role model for many. Every challenge she encounters is met with the same grace and poise she exhibits on the dance floor, turning obstacles into opportunities for growth and inspiration.

Empowering the Next Generation

One of Amy's greatest passions is empowering the next generation of dancers. She is developing a mentorship program through Art in Motion, aimed at young dancers who show promise but may lack the resources or guidance to reach their full potential. This program will offer scholarships, personalized coaching, and opportunities to perform in professional settings. Amy's own journey is a testament to the power of mentorship and support, and she is dedicated to giving back by helping others achieve their dreams.

A New Dance Production

In an exciting development, Amy has begun working on a new dance production that will tour various theaters around the UK. This production, tentatively titled "Dance of Life," will weave together her personal story with broader themes of resilience and hope. It will feature a mix of professional dancers and young talents from her dance school, showcasing the transformative power of dance. Amy is deeply involved in every aspect of the production, from choreography to costume design, ensuring that it reflects her vision and message.

Advocacy and Awareness Campaigns

Amy's advocacy efforts are reaching new heights. She is collaborating with major health organizations to launch nationwide campaigns aimed at raising awareness about Crohn's disease and breast cancer. These campaigns will include public service announcements, social media initiatives, and community events designed to educate the public and support those affected by these conditions. Amy's personal experience lends authenticity and urgency to these efforts, helping to break down stigmas and encourage early detection and treatment.

Expanding Digital Presence

In addition to her in-person engagements, Amy is expanding her digital presence. She plans to launch a YouTube channel and a podcast where she can share dance tutorials, health tips, and personal insights. These platforms will allow her to connect with a global audience, offering inspiration and guidance to people from all walks of life. Amy's content will be a mix of professional dance instruction and candid discussions about her journey, providing a well-rounded view of her life and passions.

A Lifelong Journey of Learning

Despite her numerous achievements, Amy remains committed to lifelong learning. She is considering pursuing advanced studies in dance therapy, combining her love for dance with her desire to help others heal. This new field would allow her to explore the therapeutic benefits of dance, offering a unique perspective that blends artistry with health and wellness. Amy's curiosity and willingness to evolve are key aspects of her enduring success and influence.

The Power of Community
Amy's story is a powerful testament to the importance of community. From her supportive family and friends to her loyal fans and dedicated students, the people in Amy's life have played an integral role in her success. She often speaks about the strength she draws from these connections, emphasizing that her journey is a collective one. This sense of community is something Amy actively fosters, creating environments where people feel valued, supported, and inspired.

Continuing to Inspire
As Amy Dowden looks to the future, her vision is clear: to continue inspiring others through dance, advocacy, and personal storytelling. She remains committed to using her platform for good, bringing light and hope to those who need it most. Amy's journey is a testament to the power of resilience, passion, and the human spirit's capacity to triumph over adversity.

Conclusion
Amy Dowden's life is a remarkable narrative of passion, perseverance, and inspiration. Her journey from a young girl in Caerphilly to a celebrated dancer and advocate is a beacon of hope for many. Amy's story continues to evolve, filled with new ventures, challenges, and triumphs. As she dances into the future, her legacy of strength, love, and resilience will undoubtedly continue to inspire and uplift, proving that with determination and heart, anything is possible.

A Global Impact

Amy Dowden's influence extends far beyond the dance floor. Her commitment to advocacy and empowerment has made her a respected figure not only in the world of dance but also in health and wellness communities worldwide. As she continues to expand her reach, Amy's impact grows, touching the lives of individuals across the globe.

International Advocacy Efforts

Amy's collaboration with health organizations has taken her advocacy efforts to an international level. She is involved in campaigns and initiatives aimed at raising awareness about Crohn's disease and breast cancer on a global scale. Through speaking engagements, media appearances, and partnerships with international organizations, Amy amplifies her message of hope and resilience to audiences around the world. Her tireless advocacy work is making a significant impact in destigmatizing these conditions and promoting early detection and treatment.

Cultural Exchange Through Dance
Amy is also passionate about using dance as a tool for cultural exchange and understanding. She has embarked on international dance tours, collaborating with artists and dancers from diverse backgrounds. These tours not only showcase the universal language of dance but also foster connections and friendships across borders. Through her performances and workshops, Amy promotes cultural diversity and mutual respect, emphasizing the power of dance to bridge differences and unite people from all walks of life.

Philanthropic Endeavors
In addition to her advocacy work, Amy is deeply committed to philanthropy. She is involved in various charitable initiatives, supporting causes close to her heart, such as children's education, healthcare, and environmental conservation. Amy's generosity extends to local communities as well as global initiatives, demonstrating her dedication to making a positive impact wherever she goes. Her charitable efforts inspire others to give back and make a difference in the world.

Mentorship and Leadership
Amy's role as a mentor and leader continues to grow as she takes on new responsibilities within the dance community. She is actively involved in mentoring young dancers, providing guidance, support, and encouragement as they navigate their own paths. Through leadership roles in dance organizations and educational institutions, Amy advocates for inclusivity, diversity, and excellence in dance. Her mentorship and leadership inspire future generations of dancers to pursue their dreams with passion and integrity.

Legacy of Inspiration
As Amy Dowden's journey unfolds, her legacy of inspiration grows stronger with each step. Her unwavering dedication to dance, advocacy, and philanthropy serves as a beacon of hope for millions of people around the world. Through her resilience, compassion, and leadership, Amy continues to uplift and empower others, leaving an indelible mark on the hearts and minds of all who have the privilege of knowing her.

Conclusion
Amy Dowden's story is one of courage, compassion, and resilience. From her humble beginnings in Caerphilly to her global impact as a dancer, advocate, and philanthropist, Amy's journey is a testament to the power of passion and perseverance. As she continues to dance through life's challenges, Amy remains an inspiration to all who have the honor of following in her footsteps. Her legacy will endure for generations to come, reminding us that with love, determination, and a generous heart, anything is possible.

Printed in Great Britain
by Amazon